50 Meal Recipes to Boost Your Breast Milk Production:

Give Your Body the Right Foods to Help You Generate High Quality Breast Milk Fast

By

Joe Correa CSN

COPYRIGHT

© 2016 Live Stronger Faster Inc.

All rights reserved

Reproduction or translation of any part of this work beyond that permitted by section 107 or 108 of the 1976 United States Copyright Act without the permission of the copyright owner is unlawful.

This publication is designed to provide accurate and authoritative information in regard to the subject matter covered. It is sold with the understanding that neither the author nor the publisher is engaged in rendering medical advice. If medical advice or assistance is needed, consult with a doctor. This book is considered a guide and should not be used in any way detrimental to your health. Consult with a physician before starting this nutritional plan to make sure it's right for you.

ACKNOWLEDGEMENTS

This book is dedicated to any and all mothers who are pregnant or who have just had a baby.

50 Meal Recipes to Boost Your Breast Milk Production:

Give Your Body the Right Foods to Help You Generate High Quality Breast Milk Fast

By

Joe Correa CSN

CONTENTS

Copyright

Acknowledgements

About The Author

Introduction

50 Meal Recipes to Boost Your Breast Milk Production: Give Your Body the Right Foods to Help You Generate High Quality Breast Milk Fast

Additional Titles from This Author

ABOUT THE AUTHOR

After years of Research, I honestly believe in the positive effects that proper nutrition can have over the body and mind. My knowledge and experience has helped me live healthier throughout the years and which I have shared with family and friends. The more you know about eating and drinking healthier, the sooner you will want to change your life and eating habits.

Nutrition is a key part in the process of being healthy and living longer so get started today. The first step is the most important and the most significant.

INTRODUCTION

50 Meal Recipes to Boost Your Breast Milk Production: Give Your Body the Right Foods to Help You Generate High Quality Breast Milk Fast

By Joe Correa CSN

Proper nutrition is the fundamental component in establishing good lactation. Lactogenic foods, also called galactagogues, facilitate milk production by increasing certain hormones that stimulate the release of breast milk. Some galactagogues, due to their very high water content, promote hydration that brings about efficiency in milk production.

This book will provide you with simple and easy recipes that anybody can prepare in very little time so that your body can have the necessary vitamins and minerals to stimulate breast milk production fast.

Certain foods also help regulate mood. Studies have found that high stress levels can cause a drop in prolactin levels, which is the principal hormone in promoting milk synthesis and secretion so it's important to stay relaxed.

Mechanical stimulation coming from the baby is also essential in milk production. Proper latching and sucking of an infant on the mother's breasts stimulates the oxytocin hormone to release more milk from the mammary tissues. Rich, flavorful, and nutritiously-packed breast milk may expectedly result in better lactogenesis. This book is packed with galactogogues widely and/or traditionally used that is sure to delight any nursing mother!

50 Meal Recipes to Boost Your Breast Milk Production: Give Your Body the Right Foods to Help You Generate High Quality Breast Milk Fast

1. Red clover egg drop

Red clover is a good source of isoflavones which have estrogen-like properties that help stimulate milk production. Studies show that red clover stimulates prolactin secretion, therefore increasing breast milk production.

Ingredients:

- 3 Tbsp. Red clover leaf, chopped
- 1 Medium size egg
- 1 cube Chicken bouillon
- 1 Tbsp. Onion, chopped
- 1 Tbsp. Olive oil
- 4 cups Water
- Salt and pepper to taste

How to prepare:

Sauté the onion in olive oil until tender. Stir in the chopped red clover leaves. Add water and bring to a boil over a medium heat. In a separate bowl, whisk an egg and slowly pour into the red clover-water mixture. Stir lightly until the egg turns fluffy. Turn off the heat and season with salt and pepper.

Serves: 3

- Serving size: 340g

Amount per Serving:

Total Calories: 66

Total fat: 6.3g

Total carbohydrates: .7g

Protein: 2.1g

Vitamins: Vitamin A 1%, Calcium 2%, Iron 2%

Minerals: Sodium 328mg, Potassium 32mg

High in: Selenium

2. Turkey salad with poppy seeds

Turkey is an excellent choice for a diet rich in protein and low in fat. Turkey provides iron, vitamin B and selenium which are vitamins commonly deficient among nursing mothers.

Ingredients:

- 1 cup Turkey, diced and already cooked
- 1 tsp Lemon juice
- 2 Tbsp. Olive oil
- 1 Tbsp. Poppy seeds
- 2 heads of Romaine lettuce

How to prepare:

In a medium bowl, mix the poppy seeds, lemon juice and olive oil. Add the turkey and mix until the turkey is completely covered in the poppy seeds and olive oil mixture. Toss in the romaine lettuce, mix and enjoy!

Serves: 3 • Serving size: 277g

Amount per Serving:

Total Calories: 205

Total fat: 13.4g

Total carbohydrates: 7.2g

Protein: 15.2g

Vitamins: Vitamin A 0% • Vitamin C 18% • Calcium 5% • Iron 60%

Minerals: Sodium 45mg, Potassium 466mg

High: Iron, selenium vitamin B6, vitamin B12

3. Brownies with brewer's yeast

Brewer's yeast is a fungus loaded with essential nutrients, such as iron, Vit B, B12, protein chromium and selenium. It is known to help mothers increase breast milk and to regulate mood to fight off postpartum depression.

Ingredients:

- 1/2 cup Butter
- 2 Eggs
- 1 tsp. Vanilla extract

Dry Ingredients:

- 1 ½ cup Sugar
- ½ cup Cocoa powder
- 1 ½ cup Flour
- ½ tsp. Baking Powder
- ½ tsp. salt
- 1 Tbsp. Brewer's yeast

Preparation:

Preheat the oven in 350°F.

Using a blender, mix the butter, sugar, and vanilla extract. Blend well. Add the eggs and continue blending. In a separate bowl, mix the remaining dry ingredients. Mix with the butter mixture. Pour into a greased 9x9 square pan. Bake for approximately 20 minutes.

Serves: 5 • Serving size: 148g

Amount per Serving:

Total Calories: 571

Total fat: 21.7g

Total carbohydrates: 93.8g

Protein: 7.8g

Vitamins: Vitamin A 13% • Calcium 5% • Iron 19%

Minerals: Sodium 391mg, Potassium 337mg

High: Dietary fiber, iron, niacin, pantothenic acid, phosphorus, potassium, riboflavin, selenium, thiamin, vitamin B, zinc

4. Chocolate cake with fenugreek

Fenugreek is a widely known herbal remedy in boosting breast milk production. It works by increasing prolactin levels.

Ingredients:

- 1 cup Milk
- ¾ cup Canola oil
- 1 tsp. Vanilla extract
- 3 Large eggs

Dry ingredients:

- 2 tsp. Fenugreek seed
- 2 cups Sugar
- 2 cups Flour
- 1 cup Cocoa
- 2 tsp. Baking powder
- 1 tsp. Baking soda
- ½ tsp. Salt

Preparation:

Preheat the oven in 350°F.

In a large bowl, mix the sugar, flour, cocoa, baking powder, baking soda, salt and fenugreek seed. Stir, then add the remaining ingredients. Mix well for around 2 minutes or until the consistency of the batter becomes smooth.

Pour the batter in a 13x9 inch greased pan. Bake for 35-40 min.

Serves: 6 • Serving size: 190g

Amount per Serving:

Total Calories: 641

Total fat: 29.2g

Total carbohydrates: 94.4g

Protein: 10.0g

Vitamins: Vitamin A 2% • Calcium 14% • Iron 25%

Minerals: Sodium 399mg, Potassium 549mg

5. Bottle gourd meatball

Bottle Gourd is an easy to digest vegetable that increases breast milk production. It keeps a nursing mother hydrated due to its high water content. It also normalizes postpartum blood sugar levels.

Ingredients:

Meatball:

- 1 Egg
- 500 g. Ground pork
- ½ cup Breadcrumbs
- 2 Tbsp. Garlic, minced
- 1 Tbsp. Onion, minced
- 2/3 cup Bottle gourd, finely chopped
- ½ cup Carrots
- 1 Tsp. Salt
- Olive oil for frying

Tomato sauce:

- 1 Tbsp. Garlic, chopped
- 1 Tbsp. Onion, minced

- 1 can 400g. Tomato sauce
- 2 cans 400 g. Chopped tomatoes
- 2 Tsp. Tomato paste
- 1 Tbsp. Dried oregano leaves for garnish

Preparation:

Combine all meatball ingredients and mix. Use your hands oiled with cooking oil to incorporate the batter completely. Form into round balls with 2-3 inches diameter. Deep fry. Strain excess oil and put on a plate.

Tomato sauce:

Over a medium heat, sauté the garlic until golden brown. Sauté the onions until translucent. Pour in the cans of chopped tomatoes, tomato sauce and tomato paste. Reduce heat and simmer for 10 minutes. Serve on top of the meatballs and garnish with oregano leaves.

Serves: 4 • Serving size: 305g

Amount per Serving:

Total Calories: 360

Total fat: 20.0g

Total carbohydrates: 22.4g

Protein: 23.8g

Vitamins: Vitamin A 77% • Calcium 8% • Iron 17% • Vitamin C 38%

Minerals: Sodium 814mg, Potassium 894mg

High: Niacin, selenium, thiamin, vitamin A, vitamin B6, vitamin C

6. Breaded fried chicken with poppy seeds

Poppy seed stimulates the milk let-down reflex by helping mothers relax.

Ingredients:

- 500 g. Chicken breast
- Canola oil for deep frying

Breading mixture:

- 1/4 cup Flour
- 1 Tbsp. Poppy seeds
- ½ tsp. Salt
- ½ tsp. Pepper
- 1 Egg, whisked

Preparation:

Mix all breading ingredients. Dredge the chicken breast into the breading mixture. Deep fry over medium heat until golden brown. Pat dry on a paper towel to remove excess oil.

Serves: 3 • Serving size: 232 g

Amount per Serving:

Total Calories: 670

Total fat: 45.2g

Total carbohydrates: 9.0g

Protein: 57.1g

Vitamins: Vitamin A 1% • Calcium 0% • Iron 18% • Vitamin C 8%

Minerals: Sodium 601mg, Potassium 479mg

High: Niacin, selenium, vitamin B6

7. Fennel pudding

Fennel is an herb that tastes like anise or licorice. It is believed to improve breast milk supply. It is an easy to digest food that helps relieve colic in babies.

Ingredients:

- 2 Tbsp. Fennel seed, grounded
- 2 cups of water for boiling
- ¼ cup Butter
- 2 cups Milk
- 1 ¾ cup sugar
- 3 cups Eggs, (egg yolk separated and whisked)
- 3 Tbsp. Cornstarch
- 1 tsp. Vanilla extract
- ½ tsp. Salt
- Oil for greasing

Preparation:

To prepare the fennel seed infusion, boil 2 Tbsp. fennel seed in 2 cups of water. Steep overnight.

To make the pudding, first, preheat the oven in 350°F. Second, in a medium saucepan over medium heat, whisk together the cornstarch, sugar, and salt. Slowly whisk in the milk and the whisked egg yolk. Lower the heat and continue cooking for 15 minutes until thick. Add the fennel seed infusion and stir. Remove from heat and add the butter and the vanilla extract.

Lastly, pour into 6 oz. ramekins greased with oil. Bake for 35 min. Chill before serving.

Serves: 4 • Serving size: 267g

Amount per Serving:

Total Calories: 574

Total fat: 17.7g

Total carbohydrates: 100.9g

Protein: 8.8g

Vitamins: Vitamin A 11% • Calcium 20% • Iron 7% • Vitamin C 1%

Minerals: Sodium 479mg, Potassium 169mg

8. Watermelon cucumber cauliflower

Watermelon combined with cucumber and cauliflower have high water content which is essential in producing milk.

Ingredients:

- 3 cups Watermelon
- ½ cup Cucumber
- ½ cup Cauliflower

Preparation:

Juice all ingredients in juicer or mixer and enjoy!

Serves: 2 • Serving size: 279g

Amount per Serving:

Total Calories: 79

Total fat: .4g

Total carbohydrates: 19.4g

Protein: 2.0g

Vitamins: Vitamin A 27% • Calcium 3% • Iron 4% • Vitamin C 51%

Minerals: Sodium 11mg, Potassium 367mg

High: Potassium, vitamin A, vitamin B6, vitamin C

9. Creamy chickpeas soup

Chickpeas is rich in protein, calcium, B-complex vitamins and fiber. It stimulates milk production in nursing mothers.

Ingredients:

- 1 1/2 cup Chickpeas, pureed
- 1 Tbsp. Onion, chopped
- ½ cup Butter
- 2/3 cup Flour
- 2 cups Milk
- 2 cubes Chicken bouillon
- Pepper to taste
- 6 cups Water for boiling

Preparation:

To puree the chickpeas, soak the chickpeas overnight and drain. In the morning, wash the chickpeas to reduce excessive gassiness it may cause. Boil in 6 cups of water until beans are tender. Cool, then puree in a blender.

In a low heat, melt the butter and sauté the onions until tender. Add the flour, milk, chicken bouillon cubes. Stir until thick. Add the chickpeas puree. Serve while hot.

Serves: 3 • Serving size: 334g

Amount per Serving:

Total Calories: 826

Total fat: 40.6g

Total carbohydrates: 90.9g

Protein: 28.3g

Vitamins: Vitamin A 21% • Calcium 31% • Iron 42% • Vitamin C 7%

Minerals: Sodium 773mg, Potassium 1026mg

High: Vitamin B6

10. Egg salad with alfalfa sandwich

Alfalfa is high in protein and fiber, rich in antioxidants, contains trace vitamins and minerals and low in saturated fat. It contains phytoestrogens that is believed to increase milk production among lactating dairy animals.

Ingredients:

- 4 Eggs, hard-boiled
- 1/8 tsp. Turmeric powder
- 1 stalk Celery
- ½ cup Mayonnaise
- Salt and pepper to taste
- ½ cup Alfalfa, chopped in the middle of the stalk
- 2 slices Wheat bread

Preparation:

Boil the eggs for 8 min. Peel the eggs. Mash when cool. Throw in all the other ingredients and mix. Spread generously on bread and enjoy.

Serves: 7 • Serving size: 103g

Amount per Serving:

Total Calories: 241

Total fat: 10.0g

Total carbohydrates: 27.5g

Protein: 10.7g

Vitamins: Vitamin A 4% • Calcium 8% • Iron 11% • Vitamin C 0%

Minerals: Sodium 464mg, Potassium 184mg

High: Manganese, selenium

11. Grilled chicken and cheese sandwich with bokchoy

Bokchoy is rich in folic acid. It is high in vitamin B and iron which is believed to increase milk production.

Ingredients:

- 250g. Chicken breast fillet
- 2 slices Cheddar cheese
- ¼ cup Baby bokchoy leaves (stems and leaves)
- ½ tsp. Olive oil

Preparation:

Drizzle the chicken with olive oil and season with salt and pepper before grilling.

Over medium heat, butter a slice of bread and put the buttered part of the bread facing down on a pan. Put cheese on top of the bread until it melts. Transfer to a plate and layer with grilled chicken and baby bokchoy leaves on top. Using the same pan, toast another slice of buttered bread in low heat. Cover the sandwich using the toasted slice of bread.

Serves: 2 • Serving size: 161g

Amount per Serving:

Total Calories: 361

Total fat: 19.7g

Total carbohydrates: 0.6g

Protein: 43.2g

Vitamins: Vitamin A 7% • Calcium 22% • Iron 11% • Vitamin C 1%

Minerals: Sodium 282mg, Potassium 341mg

High: Niacin, phosphorous, selenium

12. Blueberry muffin with fenugreek seeds

Fenugreek seed is a popular galactagogue. It is known to stimulate the secretion of human growth hormone. It relaxes the digestive tract in babies and stabilizes blood sugar levels in nursing mothers.

Ingredients:

1 cup Whole milk

2 Tbsp. Vegetable oil

2 Eggs

1 tsp. Vanilla extract

1 cup Fresh blueberries

Dry ingredients:

1 tsp. Fenugreek seed, grounded

2 cups Flour

1 ½ cup Sugar

2 tsp. Baking powder

½ tsp. Salt

Procedure:

Preheat the oven in 375°F.

In a large bowl, combine all dry ingredients. Using a mixer, combine the vegetable oil, eggs milk and vanilla extract. Stir evenly for a few minutes. Toss in the blueberries.

Divide the batter between 12 muffin cups lined with paper liners. Bake for 30 minutes.

Serves: 8 • Serving size: 134g

Amount per Serving:

Total Calories: 333

Total fat: 5.9g

Total carbohydrates: 66.4g

Protein: 5.8g

Vitamins: Vitamin A 2% • Calcium 10% • Iron 12% • Vitamin C 5%

Minerals: Sodium 177mg, Potassium 236mg

13. Barley soup

Barley is a cereal grain that increases lactation. Due to its high water content, it helps nursing mothers keep hydrated which is important in increasing milk production.

Ingredients:

- 400g. Beef sirloin tip, chunks
- ½ cup Carrots
- ½ cup Bell pepper, chopped
- 2 cans 400g. Diced tomatoes
- 1 can 400g. Tomato sauce
- 2 Beef bouillon cubes
- ½ cup Barley leaves, finely chopped
- 4 cups Water
- Salt and pepper

Procedure:

Cut the beef in chunks. Pat dry with a paper towel and season with salt and pepper.

Combine all remaining ingredients in a crockpot. Cook in low heat for 8 hours.

Serves: 5 • Serving size: 432g

Amount per Serving:

Total Calories: 281

Total fat: 6.3g

Total carbohydrates: 26.0g

Protein: 30.7g

Vitamins: Vitamin A 75% • Calcium 4% • Iron 96% • Vitamin C 67%

Minerals: Sodium 779mg, Potassium 1167mg

High: Niacin, phosphorous, iron, potassium, selenium, vitamin A, vitamin B6, vitamin B12, vitamin C, zinc

14. Peanut butter pasta with broccoli

Peanut butter is a good source of good essential fatty acid like Omega 3, 6, and 9. Healthy fats are essential for the production of hormones, which help increase breast milk production.

Ingredients:

- 3 Tbsp. Peanut butter
- 1 Tbsp. Sesame oil
- 2 Tbsp. Garlic, minced
- 250g. Chicken cubes, diced
- 2 Tbsp. Fish sauce
- ½ cup Broccoli, chopped
- ½ cup Water
- 1 tsp. Green onion for garnish, chopped

Preparation:

To make the sauce, mix the peanut butter, sesame oil, fish sauce and garlic. Add ½ cup of water and evenly mix.

In a separate pot, boil the broccoli until bright green. Set aside. Use the same water to boil the pasta. Sprinkle salt in the water before immersing the pasta. Boil until pasta is cooked. Remove from fire and drain the pasta. Add the sauce and the broccoli on top of the pasta. Garnish with green onions. Serve and enjoy.

Serves: 2 • Serving size: 265g

Amount per Serving:

Total Calories: 417

Total fat: 22.8g

Total carbohydrates: 9.8g

Protein: 44.3g

Vitamins: Vitamin A 4% • Calcium 5% • Iron 21% • Vitamin C 39%

Minerals: Sodium 1589mg, Potassium 550mg

High: Niacin, vitamin B6, selenium

15. Macaroni and cheese broccoli soup

Dairy should be an important part of a nursing mother's diet because it provides vitamin D and calcium which are essential for the baby's bone development. It is also rich in protein.

Ingredients:

- 2 cups Cheddar cheese, grated
- 4 oz. Parmesan cheese, grated
- 1 Chicken bouillon cube
- 6 cups Water
- 2/3 cup Flour
- 1 ½ cup Milk
- ½ cup Broccoli
- ¾ cup Carrot, diced
- ½ cup Celery
- 400g. Macaroni pasta

Procedure:

Over a medium heat, sauté the garlic until golden brown. Sauté the onions until translucent. Add 6 cups of water, flour and the Chicken bouillon cube. Boil for 1-2 minutes. Lower heat and simmer until soup is thick for around 10 minutes. Add the broccoli and carrots. Continue cooking until carrots are soft for about 4-5 minutes. Add the milk, cheese and macaroni. Stir and continue cooking until cheese is melted and macaroni pasta is soft.

Serves: 4 • Serving size: 343g

Amount per Serving:

Total Calories: 745

Total fat: 29.3g

Total carbohydrates: 80.2g

Protein: 40.4g

Vitamins: Vitamin A 88% • Calcium 81% • Iron 27% • Vitamin C 20%

Minerals: Sodium 1134mg, Potassium 757mg

High: Calcium, phosphorous, vitamin A

16. Chicken in tomato sauce

Tomatoes are rich in beta-carotene which is a precursor to Vitamin A. Tomatoes are also rich in lycopene which contains the highest antioxidant measured in food.

Ingredients:

- 400g. Chicken breast, diced
- 2/3 cup basil
- 400g. canned Diced tomatoes
- 400g. canned tomato sauce
- 2 Tbsp. Garlic, chopped
- Salt and pepper to taste
- 1 Tbsp. Olive oil

Procedure:

Season the chicken with salt and pepper. Pan fry for about 5 minutes. Transfer to a plate.

To make the sauce, over medium heat, sauté the garlic. Add the cans of diced tomato and tomato sauce. Boil and stir well. Reduce heat. Simmer for 10 minutes.

On a plate, pour sauce on top of the chicken and enjoy!

Serves: 3 • Serving size: 416g

Amount per Serving:

Total Calories: 325

Total fat: 10.0g

Total carbohydrates: 14.4g

Protein: 46.3g

Vitamins: Vitamin A 37% • Calcium 7% • Iron 21% • Vitamin C 51%

Minerals: Sodium 860mg, Potassium 1134mg

High: Niacin, selenium, phosphorous, vitamin A, vitamin B6, vitamin B12, vitamin C

17. Gelatin milk thistle with vanilla ice cream

Milk thistle is commonly found in nursing mothers' tea. Studies show that it helps increase milk production among dairy cows.

Ingredients:

- 1 pack Unflavored gelatin
- ½ tsp. decaffeinated instant coffee
- ½ cup sugar
- 1/2 Milk thistle leaves, finely chopped
- 1 tsp. Lemon juice
- 1/8 tsp. Salt
- Water for boiling
- 1 cup Vanilla ice cream

Preparation:

Prepare the milk thistle by cleaning the leaves of the thistle. Wear gloves and remove the points and thorns. Wash the leaves. Take out the leaves from the midrib of the leaves. Cut unnecessary fibrous strings. Boil the leaves. Add salt and lemon juice. Stir. Cool, discard the broth and chop the thistles very finely to make ½ cup.

Boil the gelatin in 4-6 cups of water, or depending on the instruction on the package of gelatin. Lower the heat. Add the decaffeinated instant coffee, sugar, and thistles. Simmer for a few minutes until mixture is smooth. Remove from heat. Transfer mixture to a shallow tray. When gelatin is completely cool and firm, cut into small cubes.

Fill a chilled glass with the thistled gelatin and top with vanilla ice cream.

Serves: 2 • Serving size: 140g

Amount per Serving:

Total Calories: 380

Total fat: 8.0g

Total carbohydrates: 67.0g

Protein: 14.5g

Vitamins: Vitamin A 6% • Calcium 10% • Iron 1% • Vitamin C 3%

Minerals: Sodium 233mg, Potassium 149mg

18. Kale omelet with mushroom and cheese

Kale is high in phytoestrogens that is believed to promote healthy breast tissue and increase in lactation.

Ingredients:

- 3 eggs
- 1 Tbsp. Onion
- ½ Tbsp. Butter
- 1/8 tsp. Salt
- 1/8 tsp. Pepper
- 2 Tbsp. Milk
- ¼ cup Cheddar cheese, shredded
- ¼ cup Kale, brown stalks removed
- 1 Tbsp. Oil

Preparation:

In a bowl, whisk the eggs thoroughly. Add salt and pepper.

In a pan, sauté in oil the onion, kale and mushroom. Set aside.

In a skillet over medium-heat, melt the butter. Pour the whisked eggs and spread evenly. Add the milk. When egg is firm but still runny on top, add the sautéed vegetables. Cook until no longer runny, for about 1-2 minutes. Then add the cheese and gently fold the omelet in half. Serve on plate.

Serves: 2 • Serving size: 120g

Amount per Serving:

Total Calories: 251

Total fat: 8.0g

Total carbohydrates: 2.9g

Protein: 12.7g

Vitamins: Vitamin A 37% • Calcium 17% • Iron 8% • Vitamin C 17%

Minerals: Sodium 359mg, Potassium 162mg

High: Selenium, vitamin A

19. Vanilla hazelnut almond milk shake

Almond is rich in monounsaturated fats which makes nutritious and fattier breast milk.

Ingredients:

- 1 ½ cup Milk
- 1 cup Vanilla ice cream
- ½ cup Hazelnuts, ground
- ½ cup Almonds, crushed
- ½ tsp. Almond extract
- 3-4 ice cubes

Procedure:

Throw in all ingredients into a blender and blend well. Top with ground almonds and hazelnuts.

Serves: 2 • Serving size: 227g

Amount per Serving:

Total Calories: 350

Total fat: 27.0g

Total carbohydrates: 17.3g

Protein: 13.8g

Vitamins: Vitamin A 1% • Calcium 30% • Iron 10% • Vitamin C 2%

Minerals: Sodium 87mg, Potassium 408mg

High: Manganese, vitamin B6

20. Granola and walnut strawberry parfait

Oats are easily digestible and are filled with iron which stimulates the production of pitocin, a hormone which stimulates milk.

Ingredients:

- 2 Tbsp. honey
- 2 Tbsp. toasted walnuts, chopped
- 1 cup plain old-fashioned rolled oats
- 1 cup non-fat plain yogurt
- 1 tsp. Vanilla extract
- 2 Tbsp. Canola oil
- ½ cup Fresh strawberries

Preparation:

Preheat the oven in 200°C.

To make the granola, in a tray, combine oats, walnuts, honey, canola oil and vanilla extract. Mix and coat well using hands. Bake for 5-7 minutes. Open the oven and mix the granola mixture. Bake for another 5 minutes. Cool.

In a glass, put yogurt. Top with toasted granola, toss in chopped walnuts and strawberry.

Serves: 2 • Serving size: 244g

Amount per Serving:

Total Calories: 496

Total fat: 22.9g

Total carbohydrates: 57.4g

Protein: 14.5g

Vitamins: Vitamin A 1% • Calcium 26% • Iron 13% • Vitamin C 37%

Minerals: Sodium 90mg, Potassium 545mg

High: Manganese

21. Sautéed garlic asparagus

Asparagus is rich in fibre, vitamin A and K. It stimulates the lactating hormones in nursing mothers.

Garlic is also a powerful galactagogue because it stimulates milk letdown and milk flow.

Ingredients:

- 1 Tbsp. butter
- 2 cups Asparagus, cut into short lengths
- 3 Tbsp. garlic

Preparation:

In a skillet, over medium heat, sauté garlic in butter until golden brown. Throw in the asparagus. Cook evenly by occasionally stirring for 2-3 minutes. Serve on a dish.

Serves: 2 • Serving size: 154g

Amount per Serving:

Total Calories: 96

Total fat: 6.0g

Total carbohydrates: 9.4g

Protein: 3.8g.

Vitamins: Vitamin A 24% • Calcium 6% • Iron 17% • Vitamin C 19%

Minerals: Sodium 46mg, Potassium 323mg

High: dietary fiber, iron, manganese, riboflavin, thiamin, vitamin A, vitamin B6, vitamin C

22. Oatmeal with banana, honey and sesame seeds

A well-known galactagogue, sesame seed is rich in calcium. Coupled with a warm comforting bowl of oatmeal, it could cause a release in oxytocin for easier milk letdown.

Ingredients:

- 1 cup oatmeal
- ½ cup honey
- 1 Tbsp. Sesame seed
- ½ cup Banana, sliced
- 1 cup Water
- 1 cup Milk

Preparation:

Boil oatmeal in 1 cup water and 1 cup milk. Simmer until it thickens evenly. Add honey and sesame seeds. Remove from heat. Toss in slices of bananas.

Serves: 2 • Serving size: 408g

Amount per Serving:

Total Calories: 533

Total fat: 7.5g

Total carbohydrates: 113.2g

Protein: 10.8g

Vitamins: Vitamin A 1% • Calcium 22% • Iron 16% • Vitamin C 6%

Minerals: Sodium 68mg, Potassium 419mg

High: Manganese, vitamin B6

23. Sweet potato salad with cabbage and poppy seeds

Sweet potato contains phytoestrogen that promote healthy breast tissue and lactation.

Ingredients:

- 2 Sweet potatoes, diced
- 1 medium head Cabbage, shredded
- 1 tsp. Dijon mustard
- 4 tsp. Poppy seeds
- 2 Tbsp. green onions, chopped
- 2 cups Mayonnaise
- 1 tsp. Pepper
- 2 stalks Celery, chopped
- ½ cup Milk
- ½ Tbsp. Vinegar
- 1 tsp. Salt

Preparation:

Boil and cool the potatoes. Cut into cubes. Mix with shredded cabbage and celery.

To make the dressing, mix all ingredients apart from the vegetables. Pour on top of the vegetables. Garnish with green onions.

Serves: 4 • Serving size: 346g

Amount per Serving:

Total Calories: 538

Total fat: 41.4g

Total carbohydrates: 41.5g

Protein: 5.1g

Vitamins: Vitamin A 10% • Calcium 17% • Iron 9% • Vitamin C 111 %

Minerals: Sodium 1486mg, Potassium 391mg

High: Vitamin C

24. Beef with green bell pepper

Lean meat is an excellent food for nursing mothers because it is rich in iron. Iron deficiency among nursing mothers is associated with poor milk supply.

Ingredients:

- 500 g. Beef sirloin tips
- 2/3 cups Green bell pepper
- 2 Tbsp. Onions
- 1 Tbsp. Olive oil
- 1 Tbsp. Butter
- 2 Tbsp. Garlic

Preparation:

In medium to high-heat, sauté the garlic until brown and the onion until translucent in olive oil. Brown the sirloin tips. Add the green bell pepper. Transfer to a plate and enjoy!

Serves: 3 • Serving size: 209g

Amount per Serving:

Total Calories: 401

Total fat: 19.0g

Total carbohydrates: 3.7g

Protein: 51.2g

Vitamins: Vitamin A 15% • Calcium 2% • Iron 175% • Vitamin C 47%

Minerals: Sodium 140mg, Potassium 760mg

High: Iron, phosphorous, selenium, vitamin B6, vitamin B12, Vitamin C, zinc

25. Wheat bread avocado with Japanese crabstick

Healthy, high-calorie foods such as avocado is rich in essential fatty acids like Omega 3, 6, and 9 which produces nutritious milk.

Ingredients:

- 1 Tbsp. Mayonnaise
- 1 Avocado, pitted, peeled and mashed
- 4 sticks Japanese crabsticks
- 1/8 tsp Salt
- 1/8 tsp. Pepper
- 2 slices Wheat bread

Preparation:

Add mashed avocado to mayonnaise, salt and pepper. Mix well. Place on a slice of wheat bread. Layer with Japanese crabsticks. Enjoy!

Serves: 1 • Serving size: 273g

Amount per Serving:

Total Calories: 606

Total fat: 46.0g

Total carbohydrates: 44.1g

Protein: 11.2g

Vitamins: Vitamin A 7% • Calcium 9% • Iron 15% • Vitamin C 34%

Minerals: Sodium 672mg, Potassium 1118mg

High: Dietary fiber

26. Garlic and pepper steak

Iron-rich beef is loaded with energy, protein and vitamin B-12.

Ingredients:

- 400g. Steak, ribeye
- 1/2 tsp. Kosher salt
- 1/8 tsp. Garlic powder
- ½ tsp. Pepper
- ½ Tbsp. Canola oil
- 1/8 Tsp. Extra Virgin Oil

Preparation:

Pat dry and bring steak to room temperature before rubbing with salt, pepper and garlic powder.

Oil the pan with canola oil over high heat. Put the beef in the pan and cook for 3-6 minutes per side depending on the desired doneness. Transfer to a plate and sprinkle with extra virgin oil.

Serves: 2 • Serving size: 206g

Amount per Serving:

Total Calories: 431

Total fat: 13.5g

Total carbohydrates: .5g

Protein: 72.3g

Vitamins: Vitamin A 0% • Calcium 1% • Iron 38% • Vitamin C 0%

Minerals: Sodium 672mg, Potassium 677mg

High: Phosphorous, selenium, vitamin B12, zinc

27. Strawberry milk thistle smoothie

Dairy is a good source of calcium, Vitamin B12 and Zinc.

Ingredients:

- 1 Tbsp. Milk thistle seeds, finely ground
- 1 cup Fresh strawberries
- 1 cup Milk
- 1 cup Vanilla yogurt
- 1 cup Strawberry ice cream

Preparation:

Blend all ingredients and put into a chilled glass. Enjoy!

Serves: 2 • Serving size: 389g

Amount per Serving:

Total Calories: 316

Total fat: 12.1g

Total carbohydrates: 37.1g

Protein: 14.0g

Vitamins: Vitamin A 8% • Calcium 47% • Iron 3% • Vitamin C 73%

Minerals: Sodium 202mg, Potassium 610mg

High: Calcium, vitamin B6, vitamin C

28. Avocado almond milk shake

Almonds not only increases the quantity of breast milk produced, but also makes the breast milk flavorful, creamier and sweeter for the babies; thence, affecting the supply and demand, characteristic of lactogenesis.

Ingredients:

- 4 Avocado, peeled and pitted
- 1 Tsp. Vanilla extract
- 4 g. White sugar
- 1 ½ cup almond milk
- 1 cup Vanilla ice cream

Preparation:

Blend all ingredients and put into a chilled glass. Enjoy!

Serves: 4 • Serving size: 329g

Amount per Serving:

Total Calories: 696

Total fat: 64.6g

Total carbohydrates: 31.9g

Protein: 7.1g

Vitamins: Vitamin A 9% • Calcium 8% • Iron 15% • Vitamin C 38%

Minerals: Sodium 54mg, Potassium 1285mg

29. Garlic chicken spinach pasta

Spinach is rich in iron, calcium, vitamin K, vitamin A and folic acid. It contains phytoestrogens which are believed to promote healthy breast tissue and lactation.

Ingredients:

- 2 Tbsp. Garlic
- ½ cup Chicken breast, cubed
- 3 Tbsp. Olive oil
- 5 cups Baby spinach, finely chopped
- ½ Tsp. Salt
- 300g. Cooked pasta
- ½ cup Cheddar cheese, grated
- 1/8 Tsp. Pepper

Preparation:

Over medium heat, sauté garlic and chicken cubes. Cook for 3 minutes. Stir until chicken is light brown. Throw in the spinach. Cover for 1 minute. Stir and cover again. Continue cooking until leaves are wilted. Add some more olive oil if leaves have dried. Stir in cheese. Add salt and pepper. Put on top of pasta.

Serves: 4 • Serving size: 162g

Amount per Serving:

Total Calories: 409

Total fat: 17.8g

Total carbohydrates: 44.0g

Protein: 19.4g

Vitamins: Vitamin A 74% • Calcium 16% • Iron 22% • Vitamin C 20%

Minerals: Sodium 450mg, Potassium 423mg

High: Vitamin A

30. Carrot and beetroot cake

Beetroot is high in beta-carotene which is believed to increase breast milk production.

Ingredients:

- 2 ¾ cups Flour
- 2 ¼ cups Caster sugar
- 2 tsp. Baking powder
- 2 Tsp. Cinnamon powder
- 6 Eggs
- 1 cup Carrot, grated
- 1 cup Beetroot, grated
- ½ tsp. Salt
- 600 mL Sunflower oil

Frosting:

- 1 ½ cup Cream cheese
- 1 ½ cup Melted butter
- 1 cup Icing sugar
- 1 Tsp. Vanilla extract
- 1 Lemon zest

Preparation:

Preheat oven to 350°F.

Beat all ingredients used for frosting. Blend well.

Mix flour, caster sugar, baking powder, salt and cinnamon powder. In another bowl, mix eggs and sunflower oil until smooth.

Pour the egg mixture to the flour mixture. Add the grated beetroot and carrot. Grease a round pan. Pour the cake batter. Bake for 35-40 minutes. Remove from oven. Spread frosting on the cake.

Serves: 14 • Serving size: 196g

Amount per Serving:

Total Calories: 901

Total fat: 71.1g

Total carbohydrates: 62.9g

Protein: 7.3g

Vitamins: Vitamin A 47% • Calcium 8% • Iron 11% • Vitamin C 2%

Minerals: Sodium 504mg, Potassium 223mg

31. Banana chocolate almond milkshake

Almonds is rich in Vitamin E, contains essential fatty acids and is high in Omega 3 which stimulates hormones to produce more milk.

Ingredients:

- 1 cup Almond milk
- 1 cup chocolate ice cream
- 2 Tbsp. Almond butter
- 3 Frozen peeled bananas

Preparation:

Blend all ingredients. Divide in chilled glasses and serve.

Serves: 3 • Serving size: 257g

Amount per Serving:

Total Calories: 453

Total fat: 30.8g

Total carbohydrates: 44.6g

Protein: 7.1g

Vitamins: Vitamin A 6% • Calcium 11% • Iron 11% • Vitamin C 21%

Minerals: Sodium 52mg, Potassium 809mg

High: Manganese

32. Tomato moringa macaroni soup

Moringa Oleifera, considered as a super-food, is a popular herb in south Asia used to stimulate milk production. It is also loaded with iron, vitamin A, vitamin C, calcium, and potassium.

Ingredients:

- ½ cup Carrots, cubed
- ½ cup Cabbage, shredded
- 1 can Chopped tomatoes
- 6 cups beef broth
- 2 stalks Celery, chopped
- 2 cups Dry macaroni pasta
- 1 cup Moringa Oleifera leaves
- 1 can Whole tomatoes
- 1 ½ Tbsp. Worcestershire sauce
- 2 Tbsp. Brown sugar

Preparation:

Cook pasta according to its package instructions.

Boil broth. Place the cans of tomato sauce and whole tomatoes. Add the macaroni pasta. Reduce heat. Add all vegetables, cover and simmer for 20 minutes until all ingredients are soft.

Serves: 8 • Serving size: 357g

Amount per Serving:

Total Calories: 226

Total fat: 2.5g

Total carbohydrates: 39.4g

Protein: 11.1g

Vitamins: Vitamin A 41% • Calcium 3% • Iron 51% • Vitamin C 26%

Minerals: Sodium 632mg, Potassium 537mg

High: Niacin, thiamin, vitamin A, vitamin C

33. Mushroom barley soup

Barley is a commonly known lactogenic food. It contains tryptophan which is a precursor for serotonin, a neurotransmitter present in the brain, intestinal tract and mammary glands. High tryptophan levels causes an increase in serotonin thereby increasing the prolactin levels which is essential in milk production.

Ingredients:

- 1 cup Fresh Shiitake mushroom, thinly sliced
- 1 Tbsp. Onion
- 1 Tbsp. Garlic
- 8 cups Beef broth
- 1 cup Barley
- ½ cup Carrots, diced
- 2 stalks Celery, chopped

Preparation:

Over medium heat, sauté onion, garlic, carrots and celery. Cook until onions are transparent. Stir in the shiitake mushroom. Pour beef broth. Add Barley. Bring to boil, reduce heat and simmer for 50 minutes-1 hour or until barley is tender.

Serves: 6 • Serving size: 393g

Amount per Serving:

Total Calories: 180

Total fat: 2.6g

Total carbohydrates: 28.8g

Protein: 10.9g

Vitamins: Vitamin A 31% • Calcium 3% • Iron 11% • Vitamin C 2%

Minerals: Sodium 1090mg, Potassium 494mg

High: Dietary fiber, manganese, niacin, phosphorous, selenium, vitamin A

34. Yardlong beans in coconut milk

The Essential Fatty Acids present in coconut milk is important in producing hormones that regulate milk production. It contains the right kind of fat for nursing mothers because of its medium chain fatty acids, which can easily be broken down and converted to energy. The lauric and capric acid found in coconut milk also have potent antiviral, antibacterial and antiparasitic properties which protects the child and the mother from illnesses.

Ingredients:

- 4 cups Yardlong beans, cut into inches
- 3 cups Coconut milk
- 1 Tbsp. Garlic
- 1 Tbsp. Onion
- 1 Tbsp. Vegetable oil
- ½ tsp. Salt
- 1/8 tsp. Pepper

Preparation:

Sauté garlic until golden brown and onion until transluscent. Add coconut milk and boil over medium-heat. Lower heat and add the yardlong beans. Simmer for 5 minutes or until beans are tender. Add salt and pepper to taste.

Serves: 4 • Serving size: 299g

Amount per Serving:

Total Calories: 482

Total fat: 46.4g

Total carbohydrates: 18.8g

Protein: 6.3g

Vitamins: Vitamin A 15% • Calcium 7% • Iron 23% • Vitamin C 40%

Minerals: Sodium 325mg, Potassium 716mg

High: Manganese

35. Veggie burger

Black beans contain the highest amount of protein and fiber among all vegetables.

Ingredients:

- 2 cups Black beans, cooked
- 1 Carrot, minced
- 2 Eggs
- 1 cup Bread crumbs
- 1 cup Mushrooms, chopped
- 1 Tbsp. Onion, minced
- 1 Tbsp. Garlic
- 2 Tbsp. Fish sauce
- 1 cup Rolled oats
- 1 Tbsp. Mustard
- 1 Tbsp. Mayonnaise
- 4 Tbsp. Olive oil

Preparation:

Beat the eggs in a mixing bowl. Add all ingredient and mix using hands until consistency is smooth and well-blended.

Form into patties. Pan-fry until patty is golden brown or 5 min. per side.

Serves: 4 • Serving size: 234g

Amount per Serving:

Total Calories: 711

Total fat: 22.4g

Total carbohydrates: 99.1g

Protein: 32.0g

Vitamins: Vitamin A 53% • Calcium 22% • Iron 47% • Vitamin C 4%

Minerals: Sodium 968mg, Potassium 1757mg

High: Dietary fiber, manganese, thiamin, vitamin B6

36. Choco-edamame jam on wheat bread

Edamame contains all essential amino acid. It is rich in protein and carbohydrates, iron, folate, potassium, choline, vitamin K, magnesium, phosphorous, and manganese.

Ingredients:

- 2 cups Edamame, shelled
- 3 Tbsp. Extra virgin olive oil
- 2 cups Cocoa powder
- ¾ cup Butter
- ½ cup Sugar
- 2/3 cup Milk
- ¼ tsp. Salt
- Water for heating
- 2 slices Wheat bread

Preparation:

Boil edamame for 30 min. over low-medium heat.

Drain liquid. Blend in a food processor. Add olive oil and blend until smooth.

In a bowl, blend cocoa and butter. Transfer mixture into a bowl. Heat the cocoa mixture by placing the bowl on top of a saucepan with ¼ of the pan filled with water. Heat over low heat. Simmer until paste is creamy hot, but not cooked. Put mixture back in the food processor. Blend and add milk and sugar gradually until mixture is smooth. Blend with edamame. Spread generously on wheat bread. Enjoy!

Serves: 8 • Serving size: 201g

Amount per Serving:

Total Calories: 535

Total fat: 32.0g

Total carbohydrates: 55.5g

Protein: 20.3g

Vitamins: Vitamin A 13% • Calcium 24% • Iron 39% • Vitamin C 31%

Minerals: Sodium 484mg, Potassium 1092mg

High: Manganese

37. Garlic-pork coriander

Coriander or cilantro has been traditionally used to increase breast milk among nursing mothers.

Ingredients:

- ½ cup Coriander, chopped
- 400g. Pork, strips
- 4 Tbsp. Garlic
- 1 Tbsp. Olive oil
- ¼ cup Cornstarch
- 2 Tbsp. Fish sauce
- ½ cup Mushroom button

Preparation:

Coat pork in salt, pepper and cornstarch. Heat pan over medium heat. Sauté garlic. Fry the pork. Add fish sauce, chopped coriander and mushroom.

Serves: 2 • Serving size: 280g

Amount per Serving:

Total Calories: 443

Total fat: 14.2g

Total carbohydrates: 21.5g

Protein: 55.0g

Vitamins: Vitamin A 5% • Calcium 5% • Iron 19% • Vitamin C 12%

Minerals: Sodium 1511mg, Potassium 1038mg

High: Niacin, phosphorous, selenium, thiamin, vitamin B6

38. Chicken salad

Apricot contain phytoestrogens and tryptophan which naturally increases prolactin levels. It also contains calcium, fiber, Vitamin A, C, and potassium.

Ingredients:

- ½ cup Chicken, cubed
- 1/8 tsp. Salt
- 1/8 Tsp. Pepper
- 1 Tbsp. Onion, chopped
- 1 Tbsp. Olive oil
- 1 medium-size Romaine lettuce
- 5-6 Fresh apricot, pitted and halved
- 1 Tbsp. Almonds, halved

Dressing:

- 1 tsp. Sesame seed
- 1 ½ cups Balsamic vinegar
- 2 Tbsp. Garlic
- 1/8 tsp. Salt
- 2 Tbsp. Brown sugar

- 1 cup Extra virgin olive oil

Preparation:

Sauté chicken over medium heat in onions until translucent. Transfer to a plate and mix with the lettuce. Throw in apricots and almonds.

To make the dressing, add balsamic vinegar, sugar, salt and whisk. Add pepper and garlic. Gradually add the extra virgin olive oil to the balsamic mixture. Whisk continuously until well blended. Drizzle on top of the salad.

Serves: 5 • Serving size: 178g

Amount per Serving:

Total Calories: 453

Total fat: 44.7g

Total carbohydrates: 9.8g

Protein: 5.1g

Vitamins: Vitamin A 14% • Calcium 3% • Iron 3% • Vitamin C 8%

Minerals: Sodium 131mg, Potassium 203mg

39. Carrots, turmeric and honey smoothie

Turmeric is loaded with vitamins, minerals, and proteins. It stimulates lactation and prevents bacterial infection due to its antibacterial properties.

Ingredients:

- 2 cups carrots, diced
- ¼ tsp. Ground turmeric
- 1 ½ cup Almond milk
- ¼ cup Honey
- 3-6 Ice cubes

Preparation:

Puree carrots. Steam for 15-20 minutes until tender. Transfer to a blender. Add water. Puree until smooth.

Throw in all other remaining ingredients. Put in a chilled glass and enjoy!

Serves: 3 • Serving size: 222g

Amount per Serving:

Total Calories: 393

Total fat: 28.6g

Total carbohydrates: 37.3g

Protein: 3.4g

Vitamins: Vitamin A 245% • Calcium 5% • Iron 13% • Vitamin C 13%

Minerals: Sodium 70mg, Potassium 569mg

High: Manganese, vitamin A

40. Chicken glazed in barbecue topped with crushed cashews

Cashew is rich in essential fatty acids and monounsaturated fats which help produce more nutritious and fattier breast milk.

Ingredients:

- 2 Tbsp. Cashews, crushed
- 1 Tbsp. Onion, minced
- 300g. Chicken breast
- 2 Tbsp. Olive oil
- Parsley for garnish
- Salt and pepper to taste

Barbecue sauce:

- 3/4 cup Ketchup
- ¼ cup Brown sugar
- 1 Tbsp. vinegar
- 1 Tbsp. Worcestershire
- 2 tsp. Paprika
- 2 Tbsp. Butter

- 2 Tbsp. Onion, minced
- 2 Tbsp. Dijon mustard

Preparation:

Mix all ingredients to make the barbecue sauce.

Rub chicken breast with olive oil, salt and pepper. Sauté onions until translucent. Pan-fry chicken over medium heat for 10 minutes. Flip and cook for another 10 minutes. Transfer to a plate. Glaze with barbecue sauce. Throw in crushed cashews. Garnish with parsley.

Serves: 3 • Serving size: 230g

Amount per Serving:

Total Calories: 471

Total fat: 24.0g

Total carbohydrates: 32.2g

Protein: 34.9g

Vitamins: Vitamin A 31% • Calcium 5% • Iron 14% • Vitamin C 19%

Minerals: Sodium 1114mg, Potassium 601mg

High: Niacin, selenium, vitamin B6

41. Creamy carbonara with beet greens

Beet greens contain an excellent amount of calcium and magnesium. It is loaded with folate,
carotenoids lutein and beta-carotene.

Ingredients:

- 3 eggs
- 1 cup Beet green
- ½ cup bacon, chopped into squares
- 1 cup Cheddar cheese, grated
- Salt and pepper to taste
- Extra virgin olive oil
- ½ cup Pure cream
- Parsley for garnish

Preparation:

Over medium heat, sauté onion until translucent, add bacon until crisp. Throw in beet greens, cook for 3-5 minutes until greens wilt.

Whisk eggs, cream, cheese and pepper. Pour mixture into pan. Stir until well blended.

Put on top of the pasta.

Garnish with parsley.

Serves: 2 • Serving size: 153g

Amount per Serving:

Total Calories: 364

Total fat: 28.7g

Total carbohydrates: 3.7g

Protein: 23.3g

Vitamins: Vitamin A 48% • Calcium 47% • Iron 11% • Vitamin C 8%

Minerals: Sodium 475mg, Potassium 252mg

High: Calcium, phosphorous, selenium, vitamin A

42. Turmeric brown fried rice with chicken and scallions

Brown rice contains hormone stimulants that can increase lactation. It regulates mood and maintains blood sugar levels. It also provides energy for nursing mothers to ensure that the required calories are present to produce the best quality of milk.

Ingredients:

- 1 Tbsp. Turmeric
- 300g. Chicken, cubed
- 1 cup Brown rice
- 1 cup water for cooking brown rice
- 1 Tbsp. Onions
- 1 Tbsp. Garlic
- ½ cup Scallions

Preparation:

Cook brown rice in a rice cooker using one cup of water for every 1 cup of rice. Cool.

In a pan, over medium heat, sauté garlic and onions. Add chicken and cook for 5-6 minutes. Add the turmeric powder and stir in the brown rice. Stir until completely blended. Add the scallions and stir for a while until leaves turn dark green. Transfer in a serving platter. Enjoy while hot.

Serves: 3 • Serving size: 267g

Amount per Serving:

Total Calories: 399

Total fat: 5.0g

Total carbohydrates: 52.2g

Protein: 34.4g

Vitamins: Vitamin A 4% • Calcium 6% • Iron 18% • Vitamin C 8%

Minerals: Sodium 72mg, Potassium 477mg

High: Manganese, niacin

43. Fried banana split with pistachios

Pistachios are rich iron, folate, calcium, fiber, vitamin E, carotene and potassium. It also contains monounsaturated fatty acids and omega-3 fatty acid that are essential in baby's brain development.

Ingredients:

- 2-3 Bananas, sliced into halves, then lengthwise
- 1 scoop Vanilla ice cream
- 1 scoop Strawberry ice cream
- ½ cup Pistachios
- 1 cup Flour
- 2 Tbsp. Sugar
- 1 tsp. Baking powder
- 1 egg
- ½ cup Chocolate syrup

Preparation:

Whisk the egg, flour, sugar and baking powder. Dredge the bananas into the mixture. Deep fry for 6 minutes and transfer to a plate.

Scoop the strawberry and vanilla ice cream and put them on the sides. Place the chocolate syrup on top.

Serves: 3 • Serving size: 316g

Amount per Serving:

Total Calories: 647

Total fat: 15.4g

Total carbohydrates: 119.9g

Protein: 13.0g

Vitamins: Vitamin A 9% • Calcium 20% • Iron 23% • Vitamin C 18%

Minerals: Sodium 171mg, Potassium 1014mg

44. Mango banana cucumber flax seed smoothie

Flax seed is a rich source of alpha-linolenic acid (ALA) thereby increasing the ALA content of the breast milk. It is partially converted into fatty acids such as docosahexaenoic acid (DHA) and eicosapentaenoic acid (EPA). Fatty acids are said to increase milk supply. It is also loaded with folate, magnesium, potassium, vitamin E, vitamin B-6, copper and zinc.

Ingredients:

- ½ cup Cucumber
- 2 Mango
- 1-2 Tbsp. Flax seed
- ½ cup Honey
- 1 Banana
- 1 cup Plain Yogurt

Preparation:

Blend all ingredients and enjoy!

Serves: 2 • Serving size: 296g

Amount per Serving:

Total Calories: 420

Total fat: 2.8g

Total carbohydrates: 93.9g

Protein: 8.7g

Vitamins: Vitamin A 3% • Calcium 24% • Iron 9% • Vitamin C 12%

Minerals: Sodium 91mg, Potassium 609mg

High: Vitamin B6

45. Blueberry kale smoothie

Blueberry is charged with antioxidants. It also contains vitamins and minerals that boost lactation.

Ingredients:

- 1 cup Blueberry
- 2 cups Kale, washed and chopped
- 1 cup Plain yogurt
- 3-6 Ice cubes

Preparation:

Blend all ingredients and enjoy!

Serves: 2 • Serving size: 262g

Amount per Serving:

Total Calories: 162

Total fat: 1.8g

Total carbohydrates: 26.1g

Protein: 9.5g

Vitamins: Vitamin 207% • Calcium 31% • Iron 12% • Vitamin C 155%

Minerals: Sodium 115mg, Potassium 671mg

High: Calcium, manganese, phosphorous, potassium, riboflavin, vitamin A, vitamin B6, vitamin C

46. Chicken walnut salad

Walnuts are healthy, high-calorie foods that supply the demand in calories to produce milk. It also contains essential fatty acids like Omega 3, 6 and 9.

Ingredients:

- 1/2 cup Walnut, chopped
- 300g. Chicken breast, grilled
- ½ cup Cherry tomatoes
- 2/3 cup Mayonnaise
- 1/3 cup Sour cream
- 1 Tbsp. Olive oil
- 1 head medium Romaine lettuce

Preparation:

Rub olive oil, salt, and pepper on the chicken then grill. Shred using forks. Set aside.

For the sauce, mix the mayonnaise and sour cream until well blended.

Mix all other ingredients together with the sauce and shredded chicken in a bowl. Finish by throwing in walnuts on top and enjoy!

Serves: 4 • Serving size: 310g

Amount per Serving:

Total Calories: 466

Total fat: 32.8g

Total carbohydrates: 16.6g

Protein: 29.6g

Vitamins: Vitamin 8% • Calcium 5% • Iron 29% • Vitamin C 16%

Minerals: Sodium 384mg, Potassium 546mg

High: Niacin, vitamin B6

47. Roasted chicken with lemon and dill

Dill, a galactagogue is rich in fibre, vitamin A, C, folic acid, antioxidants, and minerals.

Ingredients:

- 4 Chicken breast fillet
- ½ cup dill
- ½ tsp. Lemon juice
- ½ cup Parsley
- 1 cup Carrot, sliced into strips
- ½ tsp. Salt
- 1 clove Garlic
- 2 Tbsp. Onion
- ½ tsp. Pepper
- 2 Tbsp. Olive oil

Preparation:

Butterfly-cut or split open each chicken into half. Season the chicken with salt and pepper. Sear the chicken for 3 minutes on each side until 90% cooked. Transfer to a plate.

In the same pan, add another tablespoon of Olive oil. Sauté garlic until brown and onion is translucent. Add the carrots, parsley, dill and lemon juice. Scrape the bottom of the pan for more flavorful sauce. Remove from fire. Place on top of the chicken breasts.

Serves: 3 • Serving size: 210g

Amount per Serving:

Total Calories: 350

Total fat: 15.5g

Total carbohydrates: 9.9g

Protein: 42.9g

Vitamins: Vitamin 150% • Calcium 19% • Iron 36% • Vitamin C 35%

Minerals: Sodium 556mg, Potassium 797mg

High: Niacin, selenium, vitamin A, vitamin B6

48. Moringa corn soup

Moringa Oleifera, considered as a super-food, is a popular herb in south Asia used to stimulate milk production. It is also loaded with iron, vitamin A, vitamin C, calcium, and potassium.

Ingredients:

- 1 cup Moringa Oleifera leaves
- ½ cup Corn
- 6 cups chicken broth
- 1 Tbsp. Onions
- 1 Egg

Preparation:

Over medium heat, sauté garlic until brown and onions are translucent. Add the chicken broth. Bring to boil. Add moringa leaves and corn. Boil for 3 minutes. Lower heat, put the egg and simmer for another minute or two.

Serves: 4 • Serving size: 393g

Amount per Serving:

Total Calories: 90

Total fat: 3.3g

Total carbohydrates: 5.4g

Protein: 9.2g

Vitamins: Vitamin 1% • Calcium 2% • Iron 8% • Vitamin C 2%

Minerals: Sodium 1161mg, Potassium 373mg

High: Niacin, iron, manganese, phosphorous, potassium, vitamin B6

49. Melon moringa milk shake

The superfood Moringa Oleifera, contains more vitamin C than a piece of orange beneficial for a nursing mother's immune system. It also contains 25 times more iron than a serving of spinach, which prevents iron deficiency anemia among mothers. The leaves of the Moringa also contains 4 times the fiber of oats.

Ingredients:

- 2 Tbsp. Moringa oleifera, dried leaves
- 3-4 Tbsp. Honey
- 2 cups Melon
- 3-4 Ice cubes

Preparation:

Blend all ingredients and enjoy!

Serves: 1 • Serving size: 375g

Amount per Serving:

Total Calories: 298

Total fat: 0.6g

Total carbohydrates: 77.4g

Protein: 2.8g

Vitamins: Vitamin 211% • Calcium 3% • Iron 5% • Vitamin C 191%

Minerals: Sodium 52mg, Potassium 866mg

High: Vitamin A, vitamin C

50. Creamy mung beans

Mung beans are rich in protein, folic acid, vitamin B1 and calcium which are essential in producing nutritious breast milk.

Ingredients:

- 2 1/2 cup Mung beans
- 2 oz. Chicken, minced
- 1 Tbsp. Garlic
- 1 Tbsp. Onion
- 8 cups of water
- Salt and pepper to taste

Preparation:

Sauté garlic, onion and chicken until for about 4 minutes. Add water and mung beans. Bring to boil. Lower the heat. Add salt and pepper to taste. Serve hot.

Serves: 6 • Serving size: 415g

Amount per Serving:

Total Calories: 316

Total fat: 1.3g

Total carbohydrates: 54.6g

Protein: 23.4g

Vitamins: Vitamin A 2% • Calcium 13% • Iron 33% • Vitamin C 8%

Minerals: Sodium 29mg, Potassium 1104mg

High: Dietary fiber, iron, magnesium, phosphorous, thiamin

ADDITIONAL TITLES FROM THIS AUTHOR

70 Effective Meal Recipes to Prevent and Solve Being Overweight: Burn Fat Fast by Using Proper Dieting and Smart Nutrition

By

Joe Correa CSN

48 Acne Solving Meal Recipes: The Fast and Natural Path to Fixing Your Acne Problems in Less Than 10 Days!

By

Joe Correa CSN

41 Alzheimer's Preventing Meal Recipes: Reduce or Eliminate Your Alzheimer's Condition in 30 Days or Less!

By

Joe Correa CSN

70 Effective Breast Cancer Meal Recipes: Prevent and Fight Breast Cancer with Smart Nutrition and Powerful Foods

By

Joe Correa CSN

www.ingramcontent.com/pod-product-compliance
Lightning Source LLC
Chambersburg PA
CBHW070151080526
44586CB00015B/1943